The Soul Letters You

Book 1: Letters From The ...

'Letters From The Wound' is BOOK I of the series
'The Soul Letters You Never Received', which includes
3 books.
It is the beginning of a journey Home.

Book production: New Age Publishing

Manchester

M29 8LU

All enquiries must be submitted to.... www.newagepublishing.co.uk

IBSN: 9781674793405

About the Author

Natacha Dauphin is a singer, songwriter, singing therapist, author, player of medicine drums and shruti boxes. She grew up speaking French and English in Provence, France, where most of her family still is. She now lives in York, UK with her partner and cat. She loves walking in nature, dipping her feet in the sea, drinking coffee, stroking cats, eating fresh figs off the tree. She adores the moon, the scent of flowers, colourful notebooks, receiving and writing letters and ... massive hugs.

She strongly dislikes being accused of something she hasn't said or done, frowns at the smell of fishy fish and at the sight of dodgy politicians. But most of all, she hates being told what to do (apart from when she is feeling very indecisive!).

All her creations are an attempt to capture life's offerings and mysteries. Her wish is to inspire others to recognize and honour their own inner flame and follow their dreams.

She strongly believes in miracles, in creativity and in the power of the human heart.

You can find her here:

honouringyourcreativefire@gmail.com

www.natachadauphin.com - Her blog, 'Honouring Your Creative Fire'

youtube.com/c/NatachaDauphin - Her Youtube channel with her original songs and videos

https://www.facebook.com/natachadauphin

https://twitter.com/natacha_dauphin

https://www.instagram.com/natachadauphin/

Author's Note

I am not here to fix or change you.

I am here to remind you to stop

Abandoning yourself.

Dear Reader,

This is part of my story but perhaps this is also a bit part of your story.

I strongly believe that life never punishes us, it just encourages us to fully embrace our most beautiful and unique essence.

Things happen; situations, people, experiences.

Sometimes we know why, sometimes we can work out why, and sometimes we just don't know why.

And that's OK.

People say things, do things. They hurt us. We get hurt.

We say things, do things. We hurt others. They get hurt.

This happens. What we CAN do is strive to be more aware, more awake and more compassionate with others but also with ourselves.

Healing from life's experiences takes time, courage, vulnerability, integrity, humility and a lot of love. Some days, it feels like we will never get through those dark tunnels of resentment, anger, depression, and that we will never get out of these powerful whirlpools of pain, rejection, betrayal and unworthiness.

One thing I do know, is that we are always given opportunities to grow as human beings and honour our soul's purpose and visions.

We are always given a choice in how we respond to what is thrown at us. We may not find the strength to rise today but we might tomorrow and that is fine, that is good enough.
Amongst the painful experiences I carry within me, some have been transmuted, alchemized, others still have weight and substance. Some of the people involved are still present in my life, others are not.

And this is OK. Everything is OK when we stop fighting what is.
This is part of life. This is part of learning, of growing, of loving.

When we allow ourselves to truly feel all that we are feeling, when we stop fighting the feelings, we reclaim our power and our right to be. We let go of the fear that keeps us small and hidden. We re-enter our true authentic self and remember that we can only get hurt if we love and that love is worth the risk.

My path has been to learn to love myself enough to never abandon myself, no matter what life throws at me, no matter how people treat me.

My wish is that you remember this too.

With all my love,
Natacha x

A massive thank you to my dear partner, friends and family who stand by me, believe in me and let me do my thing no matter what (whether they have a choice in this last matter is another question! I am rather stubborn!). I would also like to thank all the people I have met on the way who have really seen me and have cheered me on, whether in person or on-line. You all matter. Lastly, I would like to say how grateful I am to every single person who has contributed to my funding campaign to self-publish this set of three books. You have not only made it possible financially, but you have also given me hope, courage, strength and support beyond what you will ever know.

And, to you who is reading this, I honour and celebrate the beautiful and unique person that you are. May you always be reminded that you matter, and are worthy of all of life's magic.

I wasn't intending on eloping

But there was NOTHING

My being wanted more,

Than to run free on these pages.

Sometimes I wonder,

Where would I be

If my writing had left me,

Or if I had abandoned it?

Writing is not

A luxury for me.

It is as vital to my existence

As my own breath and heartbeat.

When I don't write,

I am like a compass

Without a needle.

I write to make sense

Of what lives within,

And what evolves around.

Yet my mind screams,

"But what if All has already been said?"

And my heart whispers,

"Wouldn't the birds have stopped singing then?"

Contents

Prologue

Every year, as a child I would receive a postcard from a dear friend staying in India. The excitement this brought was such that the feeling is still present within me today. I would touch the postcard, smell it, look at it and of course re-read it for hours on end.

Many years later I received a beautifully moving postcard from another treasured soul. At the back of it, was my address and an ink drawing that had been poured right from the heart, the eyes, the hand, the witnessing, the observing. After travelling through the loving veins of the body, the sweetness of the air, it wove itself into my own heart. A scene captured with full presence and received with full presence and gratitude.

On another occasion, completely out of the blue, I received a postcard that literally shattered the walls of my heart and the dam of my river of tears. It was the most unexpected, open-hearted honouring, acknowledging and meeting of souls one could ever receive or wish for.

These postcards, I can say with certainty, changed my life in the most delicious ways; expanding my heart and reminding me of the power and beauty of connection.

Memories of many beloved letters now flood my mind and bring a smile to my face... The moment of seeing the envelope, recognizing the writing, admiring the stamp, feeling the thickness of the letter, smelling the paper, touching the embossing, reading, laughing, crying. A full sensory and sensual experience for my heart and soul.

It dawned on me that you may not have been lucky enough to receive such a card or letter. This book is my attempt to send one to you. You are worthy and deserving of a soul letter, of soul sparkles. I have found no better way to connect to all that is - including myself, you, the place I am in, the universe I long to discover, than writing. I wish for each sentence to be both a prayer and an honouring.

I am not here with revolutionary ideas to defend, clever thoughts to discuss or even an amazing story to tell. I am here to connect to that part of you that is calling you back home, that has perhaps been neglected, hidden, lost, forgotten but that is always ready to welcome and be welcomed again; that part of you that makes you feel alive.

I am your humble mirror, your humble servant, your humble reminder.

May my words be a sweet nectar for you when you feel empty.

May they be the matches you thought you had run out of when your inner fire needs rekindling.

May they guide you to the beauty that you are. These soul letters I once wrote to myself, I now write to you. **You** are worthy. **You** are enough. **You** are love. **You** are lovable. **You** are loved. **You** are supported. **You** are guided. **You** matter dear one.

Welcome to Earth. It is quite extra-ordinary here. Sometimes we just need to be reminded of how much magic there is in the world and inside of us all. So, welcome... Welcome to new words, old thoughts, buried memories, disguised feelings. Welcome to this page which holds my hand and heart. Welcome to this journey of writing which helps me be strong and invites me to show up vulnerable while my heart softens, expands, mends and finds peace. As always, I am deeply grateful for the uncanny healing power of the dance of words.

Each day our world gets rocked; a thought, a word, a conversation, an event, a behaviour, our boat tilts and we need to try and make sense of it all. Writing has saved me more than once. Every crisis, every leap of excitement, every heartbreak, every doubt I have ever had, I have processed through writing. Thinking gets me stuck, writing sets me free and doesn't allow me to pretend. Writing about the journey while trying to capture the mystery and beauty of life through words, songs and photos, never fails to excite me.

"What else is there to do?" I often ask myself.

To write is to tap into the universal heart.

This book isn't 'about' anything in particular, it is an invitation to come home, a shared inner dialogue which I hope will inspire you to share your jewels in whatever way is right for you. We all need and deserve to freely offer the dance of our heart and soul, and to be witnessed.

Dear Soul,

I have missed you - truly missed you. I'm glad to be home. Where does the essence of innocence travel once we play 'grown ups'? I am sometimes confused as to where the question ends and where the answer begins. Perhaps it is myself I am seeking when I am reaching out to you... Who will read my words and does it matter? Who will hear my songs and does it matter? Who will listen, truly listen and does it matter? Spirit is cheering me on. The stream of your breath can guide you to all answers. By following it, you reach the source of all that is, a place where the questions and the answers have dissolved into one.

Every fear, every wound, every pain, I have transmuted and survived with writing. The movement, the aliveness, the magic of the dance on the page, the release of the breath, the expansion of the heart, the vibration and resonance of the comforting sound of the tip of the pen on the paper, the rebirth of hope - the resettling into NOW. I am allowing today to be as magical as it has set itself up to be.

ODE TO...

The beater touches the skin of the drum.

Time as we know it, stops.

Fragments of story,

As autumn leaves dance in the wind

And find a place to rest on Mother Earth,

As words, thoughts, prayers

Decide to land on the blank page,

Creating a pattern amongst the chaos.

Who writes?

The heart? The soul? The moon? The ocean? The sun?
The Spirits?

I am but a channel,

Fill me with love, fill me with space, give me open arms.

The smell of coffee gently awakens the senses,

My book is born from the hips.

It is born from all the aching wombs,

From all the joyful wombs,

From mine and my sisters'.

It is born from neither here nor there.

It is born from the wound.

It is born from the crack.

It is born from the seed of hope and the watering of gratitude.

It is born from the rivers, from the seas, from the oceans and from the endless spirals of destiny.

It is born from the courage of commitment.

The strength of faithfulness.

And the embrace of flow and change.

My book is born from the belief in magic and miracles.

Experiences are neither good nor bad.

They simply shape-shift us into who we are.

Scattered words, photographs and songs as a
testimony, a mirror, a reflection of what is, a journey
home.

Back, way back to source, way back to the essence.

An attempt to embrace the infinity and mystery of
what is.

Presence, full presence.

Thoughts, words, prayers,

Planted as seeds, eager to tell their own story,

Scattered as ashes, ready to release

And free that same old story.

Yesterday I dreamt of a tomorrow... Today I remember my dream.

The seeds of my vision were planted long before I was given eyes.

It is time to water the plants of my own love revolution.

Life unfolds gently until a hurricane comes through.

After that, the unknown grows wings and takes flight with you on its back.

There are no thoughts worth having if the heart cannot feel into them.

A day within the life of a poet without poems, of a poet of life and a weaver of beauty.

A day within the life of a seeker and mystic.

I often have nothing to say as if all has already been said and is gracefully alive within the act of observing.

These words could have been letters, postcards, messages in a bottle, but here they are, in your hands.

One of my all-time favourite things is to write letters.

To take the time to pause, focus and expand all at once.

To create this instant radiant bubble in which nothing else exists but the sheer joy of writing and connecting - to self, to the other, to you, to the everlasting, universal streams dancing freely in this moment of eternity.

And so, instead of regretting what hasn't been, let me start a new tradition of letter writing again, just slightly differently this time.

I am writing to you and I must trust that this will reach you when you are most in need of a hug, of inspiration, of reassurance, of company.

Perhaps when you feel most alone. Because, this is the magic of letters, they always arrive at the perfect time.

Will you then step forward, show up, and stand naked in the magic light of an eclipse long enough to be touched by grace and create your own love revolution?

I trust you will. I believe in you.

☾

I write from the wound,

I write from the nectar,

I have discovered

That they ARE

One and the same.

I promise

To sit here,

For as long as it takes

The beauty, within the wound,

To REVEAL itself.

🥀

Love, Loss and Betrayal

One of the big loves of my life is music. I love singing and songwriting, but my relationship with singing is an odd and complicated one. A bit like a soulmate relationship that brings up all your stuff, so you get a chance to deal with it, let go of what no longer serves you, and be free.

Unlike for some people I know, singing has not always been soothing for me. It tends to mirror the light and the shadow to such an extent that at times I cannot go there.

Last year, I went through the most traumatic, painful and heartbreaking experiences on my creative path so far, when my creative, musical, singing partner and friend just walked away. This experience brought back to the surface old wounds. I had no choice but to feel what I needed to feel, allow it to move through me, give it time without falling into victimhood. I also had to make choices: become the victim of the situation, deny my feelings, pretend it wasn't happening, or sink into it all and begin to respect, honour and celebrate my life and existence whether that meant sitting and crying or feeling like a warrior in that moment. I wasn't able to sing for ages. I felt I had lost my tribe and went back to my writing

which has always been my closest, most faithful and supportive ally. We, my writing and I, have a very straightforward relationship! We never fall out of love, never push each other's buttons.
I always feel better after writing. So here I am healing from this wound and from previous ones.

☾

The things that hurt the most are the things that cannot easily be named, grasped or formulated with words - feelings of rejection, unworthiness, disappointment, abandonment and betrayal. For in a way, they are only present in our inner life, inner world and landscape. Yet, they strangle the joy out of our innocence, the colours out of our being and expression.

These feelings need a voice, a path, a river. They must move, flow, be seen, heard and felt. Then only, will they leave us alone. It is our responsibility to give them this guidance and voice. By freeing them, we free ourselves and can begin to blossom again. How CAN we witness and honour these feelings and the death process they are entangled with?

How can we ENTER their sacred dance and discover the beauty of change, transformation and transmutation?

How can we ACCEPT the invitation from the unknown to truly rise from our ashes?

There are no miracle manuals that fit all, but there IS magic and hidden treasures on the unique journey we are BRAVE enough to embark on.

🐛

☾

The love,

The emptiness,

The longing,

The pain,

The warmth,

The loss of trust,

The regain of trust,

There IS space in my heart for it ALL.

❧

☾

Some days,

There is nothing MORE

To share

Than the sorrow of eyes

That will never see.

Some days,

There is nothing LESS

To share

Than the sorrow of eyes

That will never see.

And that's OK.

❧

☾

LOCKED behind closed doors,

The breath of life

Shivers,

As the words fail to flow.

There is a weight INSIDE my chest

That I CANNOT shift.

It is the story

Of LOST belonging and misplaced worthiness.

There is a burden

Pressing,

Heavily on my HEART,

So much so, that I can no longer

FEEL

The truth living inside it.

The wisdom and courage of my people

Were CRUSHED to the bone.

The tales of long-gone abandonment

Are forever embroidered

On the INSIDE of my veins.

And yet,

I RISE.

❧

☾

Raw and vulnerable,

Such as the rising sun at the break of dawn.

Raw and vulnerable,

Such as the open wound unready to heal.

Raw and vulnerable,

Such as my heart that has cracked open.

❧

☾

Deep vein pulsing,

With the absence of you,

With the absence of me,

With the absence of us.

❧

☾

There are times

When those who had committed,

Do NOT, or cannot

Honour their commitment;

Times when those who HAD

Honoured their commitment,

Are no longer.

These are SACRED times;

Times of deep grief, sadness and acceptance.

These are POWERFUL times,

Times of realization, clarity, surrender and expansion.
❧

☾

It is our INABILITY to carry on seeing our OWN worth that breaks the heart into a billion pieces.

❧

☾

I just want someone

To take me in their arms

And tell me,

"I BELIEVE in you."

❧

☾

I am not interested in the 'WOW' and quick dump factor. Come into my life with full knowledge of this.

❧

☾

I am not a victim,

But I DO hurt,

Sometimes.

❧

☾

Dear, dear heart of mine,

I am SO sorry

It did not work out.

I misunderstood

Someone else's 'yes'

For your kind of 'YES',

Someone else's 'let's'

For YOUR kind of 'LET'S'.

☙

☾

DEEP pain,

Feelings of abandon,

Betrayal

And

Rejection

Arise

With a vengeance

When the other

EXITS

Through the BACK door.

❧

☾

Sometimes they just AREN'T

The safe and sweet haven

They set out to be.

So be GENTLE with yourself my love,

Trust that the people

Who are meant to STAY in your life,

WILL stay

And that those who do NOT stay,

Leave room

For the ones who will VALUE

The warmth and courage of your heart,

More than ANYTHING

In the world.

❧

☾

A creation is an EARTHLY incarnation of DIVINE breath.

It is SACRED and deserves uttermost love, nourishment, gratitude, respect, devotion, time and commitment.

Without these elements, it disappears into the ether until it is called BACK by the strong vision of an open and devoted heart.

🍃

☾

I am DEEPLY sorry

Beautiful creation;

I cannot look after you

On my own.

So I let you go.

Fly FREELY,

Far

And majestically,

Sacred

One.

☙

☾

This journey of letting go

Of ALL attachment and expectations

While not giving up the love...

Tell me,

What does it ACTUALLY look like?

❧

☾

Separation comes with a bittersweet taste.

Betrayal, on the other hand,

Leaves a slippery trail behind it.

Only with RAISED consciousness,

Love and discipline,

Can we avoid

Slipping and falling

Into the icy cold lake

Of resentment, self-flagellation and destruction.

☙

☽

Perhaps,

The grief that I am feeling

So deeply,

Through this experience,

Is the LOSS

Of my original tribe.

Perhaps,

I am reliving

The betrayal and the mourning

Of thousands of souls.

❧

☾

TO THOSE WHO DO NOT STAY

To those who do not stay, who fly into my heart, take residence there for a while, swirl, twirl, withdraw, and leave as if it were OK. Well I guess, in a way, it IS OK, and in another, it is NOT OK. Your withdrawal and its ripples are a mirror for me of what happens when I negate my own worth and walk away from myself. I cannot afford to do this any longer. So, thank you. Thank you for leaving and for making my original wound burn so intensely that I have no choice but to attend to it with love. Thank you for cracking my heart wide open with such sweetly disguised violence that I have no choice but to dive deep and learn how to be gentle with it, AND with myself, for two.

There is now a new light, a new perspective seeping in, which has frankly saved me from my worst demons. And although the pain can be overwhelming at times, the beauty of my heart's unwavering love and the free dancing of my soul outcast any daunting darkness. My own heart is the source from which I MUST drink.

It carries the bravest, sweetest and most thirst-quenching water and nectar I have ever, and perhaps, will ever, encounter. By diving into it, I dive into the WHOLE universe. So, thank you, and goodbye.

❧

☾

You took a turn

And left;

Left behind

EVERYTHING we had created.

The inspired dreams and visions

Which were once given to us,

Now travel through the spheres

In search of new beings,

Who can see them,

Fall in love with them,

Believe in them,

And carry them through,

To their full potential,

In a way we weren't able to.

And this is fine,

This is good,

This is exactly as it should be,

This is the cycle of life,

In full bloom.

🐦

☾

I will not fight

To try

And make

You feel

The way

I do.

❧

☾

I miss

What we will never create

Together,

But most of all,

I miss

What you didn't see

We had,

And were.

❧

☾

I am so sorry

You had to walk away.

I entrusted you

With my heart,

But you were

Too busy

Too...

Too...

⁂

☾

Through all this,

I've had to reclaim

Parts of myself

I hadn't seen

In many lifetimes.

For this,

I am DEEPLY grateful.

❧

☾

My heart

Is literally

SHATTERED

In a million pieces.

There is

A void,

Right at the centre

Of my being,

Right at the centre

Of my dreaming.

Who am I

To say

Whether this is

A good

Or

A bad thing.

It JUST is.

❧

The Journey And Blessings Of Grief

For some reason, death and I have a close relationship. Not in the sense of me nearly dying but in the sense that many close friends of mine have passed away in these recent years. I have always had a belief and inner knowing that the ones we love never really leave us. They remain here while becoming one with all that is. I remember talking to them, as a child, sensing that they were visiting. I remember a friend of mine referring to me as a gate keeper. Today, I understand a bit better what she meant.

I am so deeply grateful for my connection to spirits and to our loved ones who have passed over. I am so deeply moved by their unconditional love, presence and guidance. So, although I lost three close friends in this last year, and I won't lie, it has been tough, their ongoing presence is very much part of my life.

☾

I want to sit

In silence,

With the presence of your absence,

And the absence of your presence.

They are one and the same.

From now on,

You will feel the wind through my skin,

You will be filled with the scent of roses,

As I allow

My whole being

To SOFTEN

Into the fragrance

Of

Love,

Eternity,

And

Oneness.

❧

☾

The day

I thought

I could no longer

Live

Without your heart,

I realized

That your heart

Had ALWAYS been

And will ALWAYS be,

Within

MINE.

❧

☾

This time last week,

I was with you,

Holding

Your hand.

Today,

I am here,

Holding

Your heart.

🕊

☾

I must not judge

My need and wish to sleep,

To float in between worlds,

To travel from one realm to another;

For perhaps, this IS

Where, and when, we hang out

TOGETHER.

And I love myself

When I am

WITH you.

🐚

☽

I have no need

To release

You.

You are

Already

Free.

I am filled

With the feeling

Of our expanding

Mutual love,

Since your departure.

☙

☾

Hey, tell me,

Where do you hang out,

Now that the universe

Is your home?

☙

☾

I am fine with death.

It is the absence of you,

The absence of us,

I sometimes struggle with.

࿊

☾

I live with the blessing

Of having shared part of the journey with you.

I live with the blessing

Of having lived part of the departure with you.

I live with the blessing

That you will carry on

Infusing my life

With your love and presence.

I live with missing you,

And feeling you,

Here,

In my heart

Always.

❧

☾

Rest in peace my love,

I will keep the light on.

🐦

☽

You have long gone,

Yet, your perfume lingers on

As that of the summer rose

Giving itself

To the sun.

☙

☾

There is no despair,

No pressure

In this 'I miss you',

Just oceans

Of love,

Filling

My whole being.

For this,

I am deeply grateful.

🐦

☾

I was once

The keeper

Of your

Heart,

I am now

The keeper

Of your

Soul.

☙

☾

The echo

Of your song

Still runs, plays and dances

Through my veins.

❧

☾

The flame

Bends

Towards

Where

You

Used to

Sit.

❧

☾

I am excited,

Excited about the unknown journey

Back to you,

About the unknown journey

Back to me.

There is

No parting,

No separation,

When one is fully present,

And MET,

At the goodbye gate.
❧

☾

The cradle

Of abundance

Is rocking

Peacefully,

The beat

Carries on,

YOUR beat

Dances on,

Forever.

❧

☾

There is no need

To think of me,

All the time.

But every now and then,

When you appear in my thoughts,

I hope your angel chest

Feels a little warm glow inside.

❧

☾

The many faces of death

Keep showing up in my life,

With a smile on their face,

Reminding me that ALL is well,

That ALL is movement,

That All is change,

That the WHEEL of life is sacred,

Just, the way it is.

❧

☾

What is it

We actually sense,

When we feel

The presence

Of a loved one

Who has passed over,

If it is not love?

❧

☾

I promised you

I would speak to you

When you left for another dimension.

So here I am,

Promise held.

Ring me back, when you are free.

๛

☾

The process of grieving

Is a priceless gift,

A full palette of flavours, colours and scents.

☾

I weep,

Not just for what is lost,

But for the love that fills me,

When I think of you.

I feel no difference

Between my love for you,

And your love for me.

The for and the from have merged.

It is quite extraordinary;

Like a cool breeze,

A gentle stroke,

On each other's soul.

❧

The Return Of The Silent Ghosts And Loud Gremlins

Those distorted voices, those sabotaging thoughts, those crippling doubts and fears that try and protect us and keep us small, we all have them. It is our responsibility and duty to say hi, and goodbye, to them!

☾

Excuse my language,

But…

The Fucking Army of Gremlins

Is

Back!

🐚

☾

In this moment in time,

I am chasing muted colours.

The ghosts, they are chasing me.

The ghosts, I am chasing them.

In the twisted maze

Of yesterday and tomorrow,

The ghosts and I, we are chasing each other.

Yet at the centre of it all,

The innocence of today prevails.

🐾

☾

REVOLUTUION INSTRUCTIONS:

• Be disciplined; keep the hungry parasites of judgement at bay.

• Be aware; neutralize victimhood with celebration of self.

▢ Warning:

Judgement and victimhood are energy and creativity suckers.

Do not feed them under ANY circumstance.

If you happen to have fed them in the past, it is NEVER too late to ween them off.

After that, sprinkle them with LOTS of love.

Start NOW.

Create your OWN revolution.
꣑

☾

THE 'I AM ENOUGH' THEME!

Playing my newly acquired 'I am enough' game, I wonder...

What are the rules?

How many players?

What is the aim?

What are the strategies required?

Is it a game of goodies and baddies?

What can my first move be?

🐾

☾

"I am enough," she whispered.

"I am enough," she said.

"I am enough," she screamed.

Did she hear herself?

And the echo from the other side of the valley
answered, in the most certain and uncanny voice:

"You ARE enough."

"You ARE enough."

"You ARE enough."
❧

☾

Every dice roll,

Every move

On the board

Says,

'YOU ARE ENOUGH'.

🐛

☾

Visits,

From

Old

Ghosts,

And

Old

Pain.

I ask myself,

"What IS old pain?"

❧

☾

Be ruthless

When choosing

Who to follow,

The heart with its wisdom and courage

OR,

The mind with its fear and arrogance.

❧

☾

Do not dwell in the stories your mind makes up and attaches to situations, feelings, people.

Do not get caught in the net of the scenarios it will attempt to feed you, again and again, in order to try and take control, keep you safe and make sense of what has no real explanation.

Thank your mind for its concern, devotion and efforts.

Release what has been playing like a broken record in your head and has distorted the experiences themselves.

These particular stories are NOT your LIFE story. They are devoid of truth and integrity and when given too much attention, they become leeches rather than the healing balm they set out to be.

You DO have a LIFE story.

It is beautiful.

It is painful.

It is powerful.

It is unique.

It is universal.

It is transcendental.

It NEEDS to be shared,

But it is NOT

The one distorted by the mind.

❧

☾

Life is happening,

Just happening.

It is not happening

TO you or TO me.

It is happening

THROUGH you and me.

❧

☽

How crazy to keep swinging

From feeling not enough

To feeling too much.

This rope we hang from,

Is undoubtedly held

By our dear and faithful tricksters,

The GREMLINS themselves.

❧

☾

THE GHOSTS AND GREMLINS - The return...

Our precious ghosts... If only they weren't so silent and still. If only they would engage in proper dialogue, I would not find them so intimidating. Because, who in their right state of mind, would give any sort of importance to a white sheet that floats about and goes woo-woo-AAAAHHHHH? Even I, would end up laughing. But a still and silent ghost is something else....

A still and silent ghost does not dance around, let alone go away. A still and silent ghost stays and stares until he is acknowledged, until he sees himself upside down in the mirror.

Our job is to provide that mirror with compassion and gratitude. By doing so, we hold the space for the feelings, emotions and blockages to be touched, embraced and released from the body the ghost has made its own, our body.

Through this process, magic strikes, the gremlins sitting on our shoulder, dripping nasty words in our ear, fall off, just like that!

The mirror is inside. Let's breathe and be patient.

The steam WILL come off.

We will SEE again.

The ghosts and gremlins will go and leave us face to face with the true reflection of our beauty and uniqueness.

🐦

Darkness and Light, A Dance

We are made of the moon; we are made of the sun. We dance with one, we dance with the other. We are made of spirit; we are made of the earth. Let's dance with all that is, without censoring, without judgement or denial. All is one.

Darkness,

Is but a hug,

Holding the light,

A bit too tight.

☽

Will you be there for me,

When the leaves fall to the ground,

Or will you walk away?

❧

☾

I cried and cried,

Until

I became

One

With the flowing

River.

❧

☾

When I honour

My longing,

My heart

Smiles.

❧

106

☾

Perhaps you DO love me enough to sit with me in silence, for as long as it takes the millions of mixed feelings and confused thoughts to melt away...

Perhaps you CAN hear my heart when it feels too heavy to speak...

☾

I carry

Within myself,

Both

The wound,

And

The new seed.

❧

☾

The rock under which we try and find shelter, when we feel ashamed and not enough, does not protect us.

On the contrary, it drops its entire weight upon us.

❧

☾

Why is it

That humans

Find it so difficult

To see through the mask?

🐾

☾

We gather miscellaneous thoughts,

Come up with a few ourselves.

We then mix them all together.

To our eyes they become this sculpture,

Made of truth and stone,

To which we must bow.

You HAVE to admit,

That this is pretty delusional,

Arrogant and insane,

To say the least.

☾

Isn't it mostly fear that makes us numb?

౭❧

☾

The mind is often scared and has its own form of eating disorder which can translate as overthinking, overdoing or numbing itself in an attempt to control life and keep us safe.

Our job is to hold space for it, with exquisite tenderness, until the heart is heard, the mind is reassured, and no longer needs to scream as loud.

In that precious moment of presence, a shift occurs, and we know, that peace is on its way.

☾

The pretty wrapper

May hide a sharp and unpleasant sweet.

That's life.

And it is always worth

The risk.

🍂

☾

Resentment and bitterness

VANISH

The moment

You attend to

Your heart's needs,

And your soul's calling.

❧

☾

Enter the darkness and shadow

When needed,

But do not feed

The hungry monster

Waiting for you

To slip,

Fall,

And give in

To his pleading call.

❧

☾

Stop ruminating

On the past,

And regurgitating

The old stories,

Over and over

Again.

Write NEW ones.

You,

AND

Your life,

Are deserving

Of this.
☙

☾

They misunderstood

Who you are.

That's OK.

Keep shining

Your light.

No matter who,

No matter what.

❧

☾

There is grace in the alchemy of tears and joy.

❧

☾

To break the karmic chains,

To retrieve the eternal wisdom,

And heal the original wound,

Is the work that needs to be done

And CAN be done.

We just need to step up,

And do the work.

This is the SACRED answer to our 'why'.

🍃

☾

It is OK.

It is OK to feel what you are feeling.

It is OK to feel ALL that you are feeling.

The rage,

The pain,

The envy,

The jealousy,

The ache,

The sadness,

The disbelief.

Do not be ashamed,

Do not resist and push against these feelings.

Do not censor any of them.

The essence of each feeling is sacred.

Allow yourself to reach it, to feel its grace with, and within, your whole being.

This journey will crack your heart open, but believe me, it is a rich, honest and magical way to true healing and freedom.

☾

Velvety purple patterns

Reshape themselves

With every breath.

And yet, the electrifying density

Of emptiness

Remains.

☾

Uprooting,

Shifting,

Realigning,

Recalibrating.

☾

In order for the light to shine,

You do not need

To get rid of the darkness,

You just need

To keep the candle lit,

And the flame alive.

☙

☾

It is all there,

Buried inside of me,

Buried inside of you

– Awaiting.

❧

☾

The information was hidden, the codes kept secret.

Much was buried, long ago, but it rests no longer.

It moves, boils and gushes out from the depths of source.

NOW, now, is time to retrieve the lost treasures and offerings.

Now is the time to dissipate the distorted beliefs and realities.

☾

The buried breaths and songs

Are arising.

Listen.

I am sitting,

With the memories,

Feeling into them,

Sinking into them,

Rising with the scent they have left behind.

I feel empty, and full, at the same time;

Unbelievably empty,

Unbelievably full.

How are you feeling?

❧

☾

Do we write

To find out,

Or to remember?

❧

☾

Buried deep in my bones is the knowing, the wisdom, the key.

But WHAT are bones really made of?

How do they carry the energy, the memories, the insight, the traumas from long ago?

How is it that they are made of the essence, the question, the answer and the mystery of all that is and not just of physical substance?

I have never, until now, felt this particular connection with bones.

Something dormant has been awakened and activated.

The drumbeat is soliciting the deepest mysteries to rise out of the dark, to come forth and answer the call.

The feeling of aliveness is tremendous.

We are coming home, at last.
❧

☾

I was an orphan before I met ME.

۽

☾

Some days,

I am

As soft,

As delicate,

As inviting,

As a rose petal.

Other days,

I am

As distant,

As prickly,

As protective,

As a hedgehog.

And so it is.

All is well.

☾

There is space in my heart for wishes, hopes, questions.

There is space in my heart for the unknown, the familiar.

There is space in my heart for the magic of a fleeting moment and the journey of a lifetime.

There is space in my heart for ALL to be experienced.

❧

☽

We often blame the heart,

For leading us astray,

When it is the heart,

That leads us home,

When it is the heart,

That IS home.

❧

☾

Dance with me, when all seems lost and bare.

Dance with me, in the depths of your despair.

Dance with me, for there is no higher ecstasy

Than this meeting and merging of our energies.

Dance with me, I hear her say to me.

Day after day, as the sun goes down, my soul faithfully howls to my heart,

"Dance with me."

❦

☾

LAUGHING

I had forgotten how to laugh,

What to laugh about,

How it even felt to laugh.

Yet my body remembered belly laughs,

My soul, uncontrollable giggles,

My heart, the awesome expansion.

I had forgotten how to laugh

Until I shed the skin of protective seriousness.

☾

As human beings we can oscillate between the deepest pain and the highest feelings of ecstasy, covering a huge palette of frequencies and vibrations, in a very short amount of time.

These extremes can seem paradoxical, but they are valuable gifts on our journey towards a more gentle place of stillness.

A place where trust, love, faith and surrender rather than fear and expectations co-exist.

A place that welcomes us no matter the chaos around, and inside.

A place that is there for us regardless of who, why, how, where and when...

❧

☾

Can one touch a snowflake,

Without destroying it?

☙

☽

When our pain is unbearably deep and intense, we are either pulled into profound numbness or pushed into uncanny presence.

☾

There will always be

UNANSWERED, UNREQUITED

Love,

And

Letters...

❧

☾

What can you do when the energy that was once an inspiration for someone becomes a threat to them?

Nothing.

Keep nurturing who you are, gently and fiercely, just as the warrior of love, peace, courage and faithfulness that you are.

☾

Our perceptions are often veiled by layers of inner fog and sleep.

Know this, do not condemn it.

Do not get discouraged.

Do not give up.

Are you living in alignment with your core values?

Remember, and trust, that light can pierce through, and show you its infinite beauty and glow, at any given moment.

Be ready, open your eyes, open your heart.

Don't be scared.

There is really nothing to fear.

This light will only burn off the layers of illusion,

And dissolve what never really was.

☾

You were wanting

To spread your wings

Far and wide my love,

Not realizing that

You were taking

Your own cage with you.

❧

☾

Wake up.

It is time.

There has been enough damage.

Peel away the protective layers that have formed within and around you. They have become more dangerous than that icy path at the top of the cliff.

Put down the pair of pink glasses, stop fooling yourself trying to fix what isn't yours to fix.

Cut through the distortions, again and again, until the naked truth stares you in the eye.

Take responsibility for your own story and healing.

All will be well.

☾

If you could only love your vulnerabilities the way you love your children dear one, you wouldn't use them with such disrespect and sell them cheaply on the side of the road.

☾

There is conditioning,

And ...

There is choice

– with all matters and actions.

৵

☾

I need to find a system,

This chaos is blurring my vision.

I need to find a system,

Perhaps surrendering will ease the tension.

I need to find a system,

Boundaries and less resistance.

I need to find a system,

A system as strong as the trunk of a tree,

As flexible as a branch in the wind,

A system that withstands the storms of change,

And grows with the blessings of the sacred elements,

A system that combines discipline with freedom,

Craftsmanship with intuition,

Rhythm with flow,

Messiness with elegance,

A system that honours life to its fullest.

This system is that of the earth's cycles

In which chaos and grace

Dance, separate and unite,

To create the most beautiful offerings.

❧

The Wound: Birther of Beauty

The wound is not to be feared. She is beautiful, and perhaps the richest soil we are ever given to plant the most extraordinary, colourful and magical garden there is. If we can lean into all that she has to offer, we will not drown, we will rise with sparkles of miracles guiding us on our way.

☾

I write

From the wound,

Like never before.

I am discovering

That within it,

Lies

The SWEETEST of nectars.

❧

☾

Most miracles are born from the wound,

Held safe by darkness,

Blessed by the moon,

And courageously nurtured, by the sun.

❧

☽

What is

A broken heart,

But a heart

That feels.

☾

The heart cracks open,

At the most unexpected moments.

From the crack itself,

Exquisite and delicious honey,

Is born.

☾

"It's just the two of us this time,"

Says my heart,

As I watch it tear

Right through the middle.

"But we can do this."

"We can heal."

"We will heal."

"We are healing."

"I trust you."

"You must trust me."

❧

☾

Unplug

From those multiple extensions,

And go back

To source.

৵

☾

I will not give up.

I will not give up on me,

No matter who,

No matter what.

This is the lesson.

☾

Magic happens

With every breath,

With every step.

Trust it,

Believe it.

All is well.

❧

☾

Dear heart,

I will hold you until you are ok.

I am no longer afraid

Of loving you.

I am no longer afraid

Of loving 'me'.

❧

☾

Wow...

It feels like I am diving so deep into the wound at the moment, that a whole new exciting and enchanted world is being handed over to me, to play and explore in.

☾

May I respect,

Honour

And celebrate

My life and my existence,

Like no one else can.

☾

Reach for the essence

Of each feeling.

Within this essence,

There is no distortion,

Just deep acceptance.

☾

One day,

I will no longer

NOT

Love myself.

Maybe

TODAY,

Is

The

Day.

❧

☾

Letting go,

In this moment,

Of all need to

Prove,

Understand,

Control,

Compare,

Fix.

❧

☾

I observe the many facets and intricacies

Of what is arising,

The complexity and simplicity of what is.

Witnessing, is a fully active state.

☾

I am not giving up.

I am giving over

What I cannot understand, fix or embrace.

And for this,

I do not blame myself

I CELEBRATE myself.

❧

☾

I have thrown many golden coins in fountains,

Blown dandelion wishes across oceans of fields,

Always with the same prayer in my heart,

May I feel worthy of you dear Creator.

☽

I am ready

For the veil

To melt away,

For the door

To burst open,

For our new form of embrace

To be born.

❧

☽

In solitude, I pray for the courage to truly see the beauty I have been given, and to never stop seeing the magic all around me.

In solitude, I bow to the unwavering support and guidance I receive each day, even when I am blind, unaware and asleep, even when the feeling of being lost is overwhelming and the sense of not belonging has such a grip on me that it is almost too painful to bear.

In those moments, I know I am not alone.

In those moments, I do not pray in desperation, I pray in awe and with gratitude for the power of prayer itself.

I pray for something bigger than myself to smile and radiate through me.

I hand over to spirit what I cannot resolve on my own, what is not my duty to resolve on my own, and together, we move mountains.

🍃

☾

In this life,

I've had to learn

To love myself,

Unconditionally.

I've had to learn

To forgive myself,

For believing

That someone else's dedication

And commitment

Could, and would be,

As solid and long-lasting

As mine.
❧

☾

Let them walk away

If they cannot see your light.

Step onto the boat

That will carry your vision

To the next port,

To the next horizon.

🐦

☾

Don't ever let someone else's sudden loss of belief in you be the new standard against which you measure yourself.

The fact that they stopped seeing you for who you are, and withdrew, has nothing to do with how worthy you are.

In these dark times, may you learn to see your worth, uniqueness and sacredness more clearly than ever before.

❧

☽

Remember that if something ends, there is ALWAYS something better waiting for you around the corner, even if you can't believe or see it, just now.

Something magical and even more in alignment with your true being, vision, soul purpose and path.

"Trust," I tell myself,

"There is room and there IS a need for you, in this world, JUST the way you are."

☾

You left,

My world

Shattered,

My heart

Burst open,

My tears

Ran like a river.

And yet,

I am left

With the most beautiful blank canvas,

With the juiciest 'me' to be,

With incredible mysteries to embrace,

And many future colourful stories to dream.

☾

Your betrayal taught me one of the most precious lessons one can ever receive, to never betray myself - at any cost.

☾

I am grateful for your abandoning. It holds a mirror in front of me in which I can see how much I destroy myself and my creative fire when I walk away, neglect and break the commitment to my muse, to my inspiration, to my calling.

☾

The trails of tears and pain you leave behind will water the earth for new plants to grow.

☾

Dear heart,

Dear body,

Dear soul,

Dear spirit,

All is well.

We are healing together.

೭౿

☾

When I walk barefoot on the earth,

May I feel her unconditional support,

May I allow the sun on my cheeks,

May I smell the sap of the trees,

May I gaze at the stars and their dance,

Long enough to accept, forgive, cry,

And give myself to the moon.

❧

☾

I call upon

The waterfall

Of universal love

To clear,

Cleanse,

And

Soothe,

My aching heart.

❧

☾

Can

A simple act

Of kindness

Bring back

Someone's faith

In humanity?

❧

☾

I vow to deepen my devotion to the inspiration that is given to me.

I vow to nourish and celebrate each seed that is offered to me.

I vow to accompany its growth, and life, to the best of my abilities.

I vow to persevere when there are stones and obstacles on the path, not by pushing, but by allowing, by keeping the vision strong, by heightening my presence, by staying with it, and seeing it through.

I vow to do my best and be discerning regarding the seeds that are no longer eager to incarnate and need to be disposed of, in order for others to thrive.

I vow to honour the cycles of life and the medicine I have been entrusted with.

❧

☾

Regrouping

Regathering

Refuelling

☾

I

Forgive

Myself

For

Feeding

The wound,

Instead of

Listening

To it.

❧

☾

Laughter

Is

But

The

Rainbow

Of

Pain.

❧

☾

May I commit to not hiding.

May I commit to showing up.

May I commit to rising from the embers and ashes.

May I commit to walking my path with authenticity and courage.

May I not be ashamed of any of my wounds, flaws, doubts, values, imperfections.

May I find the will, determination and inspiration to honour my creative FIRE.

May I take BACK the power I inadvertently gave away.

May this be the full death and rebirth I was not able to have before.

May I find the alignment, connection, channel and freedom to tell the story from the wound, from the darkness, from the light born out of a heart, bursting right open.

May I allow all that is, to be.

May I feel worthy of being the bridge I am MEANT to be.

❧

☾

I will

Wake up

From this slumber,

I will

Rise

From these ashes,

Not as a phoenix

But as a cracked,

Beautiful piece

Of ancient pottery.

☾

The ecstatic breath

Of this very moment,

Is ALL I need.

❧

☾

I want to get lost in words, in music, in sounds, in drumbeats, in heartbeats.

I want to surrender, and to let go until my whole being can dance without a glimpse of censorship, edit, restriction, boycott.

Drunk and ecstatic from having touched the lips of this fleeting moment.

I want to write and play, until my eyes can no longer stay open, until my arms can no longer stay closed, until my heart can no longer harden and shrink.

I want to write and play, until I lose myself so deeply, that the distorted layers and false beliefs drop off, and I find myself naked and whole.

I want to write and play, until I can truly see myself, for the first time.

❧

☾

I have come to realize, that I am the one who must never give up on myself and my creativity.

And that is OK, more than OK.

All is well.

🐦

☾

My scream only sounds too loud to the ones who cannot receive it.

My silence only feels too heavy to the ones who cannot hear it.

My pain only seems too deadening to the ones who cannot feel it.

I am ready.

I am rising.

☾

Clearing, cleansing, reclaiming.

Ink pouring through, ink pouring out,

The moisture of the letters, the taste of the words,

The energetic dialysis at the tip of my fingers, at the tip of yours.

I sit,

I pause,

I let go,

I breathe,

I surrender.

I begin to soften and feel again,

I expand.

The comforting smell of coffee,

The gentle breeze,

It all makes sense again.

The no beginning,

The no end,

The alone - ness,

The togetherness,

The diving in,

The expansion.

❧

☾

Throughout all my wanderings and doubts,

I never ever question life itself,

And the uncanny presence

Of guidance and support

From other realms.

This, I believe

Is a deep blessing.

❧

☾

To learn to accept the contradictions, to observe without judgement what may, or may not, make sense to us, is a massive step towards fully embracing our spiritual experience in this human body, with an open heart and a vibrant spirit.

It is nothing short of AMAZING.

It is basically saying a big unconditional YES to life itself.

☾

I was unfaithful to my longing and fell into neediness.

I now let myself flow into the tender centre of the longing itself, a place of deep acceptance, expansion and tenderness.

From there, who knows where the journey will take me.

☾

I heal

The pain

Of being misunderstood,

By listening

To the beats

Of my own heart,

And the whispers

Of my soul.

This process

Enables me

To get in touch

With their humble wishes and intentions.

☾

Perhaps,

I

Can

Collect

The

Seeds,

Once

The

Flower

Has

Wilted...

❧

Epilogue

Where would I be if I had abandoned myself?

Within each moment we have the choice to either soften and expand our heart or harden and tighten it.

Within each situation we have the choice to either give in to fear, drown in bitterness and resentment or dive deep into the same fear and rise, awakened and reborn.

This choice is not about avoiding the feelings, it is about allowing them, reclaiming them, respecting them, and using them as our favourite trampoline ever.

We ALL have the power to do this.

Sitting in the dark is neither dangerous nor morbid. In fact, it can be one of the most healing things you can do. Embrace the darkness, it is OK, but keep a candle nearby, ready to be lit.

When the time is right, you will know how to welcome the flame. Life is a cycle. All parts of the cycle need to be witnessed, lived, honoured and celebrated.

Everything is movement, everything is rhythm - from our heartbeat to our breath, from the dancing of the sun, of the oceans, to the cycles of the earth and the moon. Everything is interconnected. Everything is present in the sacred echo and reflection of what is.

Words are but an attempt to describe the indescribable, the magic and the intangible. Prayers are but a longing for the unknown to take us in its arms and tell us that it is ok and that it will be ok. All of it.

What was that fleeting moment if not a shooting star?

I smile.

Perhaps a secret window into our deepest longings, overlooking the sacred plains of belonging...

What is it about windows, lights, shadows that awakens the imagination and fascinates us so much?

Is it that they are mirrors, doorways into the intricate patterns of life and the landscapes of one's own soul?

If we are made of stardust, then what are dreams made of?

Perhaps I was never meant to come to this planet, but I am directionally dysfunctional and we didn't have satnav in those days. So, might as well make the most of my time here, on this beautiful and breathtaking planet.... I have learned that one can be both a nomad and a builder, a seeker and an observer, and that most things that seem like contradictions are merely different strangely shaped pieces from the same puzzle.

I am a vessel,

I am a channel,

I am a bridge,

And so are you.

Your soul whispers, whispers, whispers with excitement.

Invite your muse... Call her ... gently... loudly... whatever it takes,

Do it 'NOW!'

Creativity is the healing bridge between your heart and your soul held up by the magic breath of spirit.

Songs, photographs, paintings, delicious food, weavings and all other creative endeavours have a flavour of magic when the essence of life is captured without being made captive - just like a rainbow, just like a butterfly.

So is your creative impulse,

So is your love,

So is your light,

So is your flame,

So is your fire,

So is your life,

MAGICAL.

Magical beyond your imagination.

The seed has been planted.

Rest now.

Come back tomorrow and water it.

Come back the next day and get rid of the weeds.

Come back after that with a heart filled with love, gratitude and trust.

From my heart to yours, from my soul to yours.

I am cheering you on.

The end is a new beginning...

Miracles await you.

Dedication

I would like to dedicate this book to all the beautiful souls on both sides of the veil, who hold my hand, have my back, believe in my dreams, comfort my heart and never give up on me - especially when the gremlins get louder than the angels.

With all my heart, Thank you.

Coming soon....

The Soul Letters Vol 2: Your Healing Balm is Waiting
For You

·

Printed in Great Britain
by Amazon

46538877R00123